to a
Better Marriage

by
Donald E. Moore

HARRISON HOUSE
Tulsa, Oklahoma

Unless otherwise indicated, all Scripture quotations are taken from the *King James Version* of the Bible.

06 05 04 03   15 14 13 12

A Daily Guide to a Better Marriage
ISBN 0-89274-554-1
(Formerly ISBN 0-88144-021-3)
Copyright © 1983 by Donald E. Moore
STEPS TO VICTORY MINISTRIES, INC.
P.O. Box 221316
Charlotte, NC 28222-1316

Published by Harrison House, Inc.
P.O. Box 35035
Tulsa, Oklahoma 74153

Printed in the United States of America.

Introduction

During the years that I have been in the ministry and have served as pastor, I have seen a great need among Christians to learn to build and protect their marriages against Satan and his devices.

Through years of experience, God has shown my wife and me how to go from defeat to victory in our own marriage. What we have learned, I have attempted to share in these pages. It is my purpose in writing this book to give encouragement to those whom the enemy has discouraged, those who feel there is no longer any hope, no need to try any more at their marriage.

The book is divided into thirty lessons or thoughts, one for each day of the month, based upon a Scripture text. At the end of each day's reading there is a prayer of commitment and a personal confession of victory in that area.

This book will not give all the answers to every marriage problem. However, I do believe that as you read these words, pray these prayers, and take your stand upon these confessions of faith from God's Word, you too will come to discover the keys to building a better marriage.

Donald E. Moore

Author of IMPROVING YOUR
        CHRISTIAN PERSONALITY

Day I
Understanding Your Partner

Wisdom is the principal thing; therefore get wisdom: and with all thy getting, get understanding (Prov. 4:7).

Having been pastor of several churches, I have met many people who thought their mate should be perfect, while they themselves treated that mate like a slave.

We must understand that our marriage companion is not perfect, cannot be perfect, and will never be perfect.

Don't try to make your companion live up to a standard that he or she can never reach; after all, you are not perfect either.

Prayer: Father, give me understanding. Help me to understand that my wife or husband can never be perfect. Help me not to try to force him or her into a mold that is impossible to live up to. In the Name of Jesus I pray.

Confession: I receive understanding from God. I receive wisdom from God. My own eyes are open to the fact that I am not perfect and my mate is not perfect either.

Day 2
The Example of Love

Charity never faileth (1 Cor. 13:8).

When a person becomes angry or confused, he has a tendency to try to force or drive, rather than to lead with love. You may be trying to force your mate into changing instead of loving him or her into changing.

The word "charity" used in this verse means love, a giving love. When we think of charity, we think of giving. Sometimes in a marriage if we look real closely at ourselves, we might see that we have slipped out of an attitude of giving love into one of a driving, forcing, "You-will-do-it-or-else" kind of attitude.

Prayer: Father, help me to lead my mate with love. Help me not to drive or force, but to love and lead by setting the example I should. In the Name of Jesus I pray.

Confession: I receive love into my heart, the giving kind of love to help my mate.

Day 3
Help, Not Criticism

Put away from thee a froward mouth, and perverse lips put far from thee (Prov. 4:24).

I find that most people spend more time complaining than helping. If you will be honest with yourself, you may find that you are complaining all the time about what your mate is doing wrong, instead of helping him or her to do it right.

Many times we find ourselves spending more time helping strangers than we do our own family. You must take time to work with our own loved ones. Take time to teach and help each other.

Even ministers fall into this trap. A pastor may help or teach others, but does he take the time to minister to his own wife or children?

I hear many men say, "I wish my wife knew the Bible like So-and-So's wife does." My question to them is: Have you taken the time to teach your wife, or only to complain?

Prayer: Father, help me to take the time to teach my own family, not harping or complaining, but helping them through their weaknesses. In the Name of Jesus I pray.

Confession: I receive wisdom, love and patience to help my mate to grow, and to learn and understand.

Day 4
A Word Fitly Spoken

A word fitly spoken is like apples of gold in pictures of silver (Prov. 25:11).

In dealing with others, we must remember that a right attitude often makes the difference between success and failure. People can feel what comes from your spirit, whether good or bad, love or hate.

Think before you speak. Is what you are about to say to your mate a fitly spoken word? Is it in the right attitude? What you say, and how you say it, may well determine whether you convince your mate you are sincerely trying to help him or her to overcome a weakness.

Prayer: Father, help me to have the right attitude toward my mate. Help me to choose fitly spoken words, words of love and kindness. In the Name of Jesus I pray.

Confession: I receive by faith help from God to have the right attitude toward my husband or wife. I receive the right words to say to him or her to overcome weakness, without causing anger or hurt.

Day 5
Trouble Not Yourselves

He that troubleth his own house shall inherit the wind . . . (Prov. 11:29).

When two people are joined together in marriage, the Bible says that they become one flesh. (Gen. 2:24.) When you fight against your marriage partner, you hurt your own self.

You will never win by taking the world's attitude of "I'll get even with you." You must understand that if you hurt your companion, you are destroying part of yourself.

As a result of fighting and bickering, homes end in divorce and the family gains nothing. Rather, it loses everything.

Prayer: Father, help me not to trouble my own house. Help me to love my mate. In the Name of Jesus I pray.

Confession: I receive help from You, Lord, to be more considerate of the one I have married.

Day 6
Forgive and Forget!

And above all things have fervent charity (love) *among yourselves: for charity* (love) *shall cover the multitude of sins (1 Pet. 4:8).*

For a real breakthrough to come in your marriage, you must learn to forgive and to forget all of your partner's past failures and mistakes.

We sometimes find this hard to do because there are some things we simply don't want to forgive and forget. Somewhere we have gotten the mistaken idea that we need to hold on to our mate's past failures and mistakes to use as a weapon against him or her in time of argument.

No marriage will ever succeed until the partners learn to forgive as Christ forgave. How did He forgive? He forgave – and forgot! Remember, "Love never fails." The weapon with which you are going to win the battle is not a carnal or fleshly weapon, but rather it is with love that you win the victory.

Prayer. Father, help me to forgive and forget as You do, so that there may be healing in our marriage and room in our hearts and minds for a fresh start. In the Name of Jesus I pray.

Confession: I receive help to forgive and forget so that God may bring healing to our marriage.

Day 7
The Love of God

But God commendeth his love toward us, in that, while we were yet sinners, Christ died for us (Rom. 5:8).

Sometimes after we have been hurt or bruised, we find it hard to let go of old wounds. If you are finding at this point that it is hard to forgive and forget, then you need to review the Scriptures on what Christ did for you.

But he was wounded for our transgressions, he was bruised for our iniquities: the chastisement of our peace was upon him; and with his stripes we are healed (Is. 53:5).

Christ died for you while you were still a lost sinner. God sent His love through Jesus Christ while you did nothing but sin against Him. He loved you with all your problems.

Prayer: Father, help me to show my wife or husband the same love with which You loved me. In the Name of Jesus I pray.

Confession: I receive help from the Lord to love, and to show love and tenderness to my mate.

Day 8
By Faith, Not Feelings

For we walk by faith, not by sight (2 Cor. 5:7).

At this point your flesh (your feelings) may not be happy at the decision you have made to forgive and forget by faith.

You cannot build a marriage on feelings, it must be built on the Word of God. You can never build a strong marriage on feelings. A marriage is a lifetime commitment. You need to commit yourself to win over the devil, and to save your marriage.

Prayer: Father, help me to put away my childish feelings and build my marriage on the written Word of God by faith. In the Name of Jesus I pray.

Confession: I will work to make my marriage a better marriage. I confess that God is helping me to overcome my childish feelings.

Day 9
Commitment in Marriage

Your adversary the devil, as a roaring lion, walketh about, seeking whom he may devour (1 Pet. 5:8).

There must be a strong commitment to build a marriage because the devil has come to destroy. He tries to divide a house against itself, because he knows it will not stand if the members are not united as one against him.

We must understand that we have to work harder than the devil. We must cast down the works of Satan in the Name of Jesus.

Prayer: Father, help me to stay committed to working harder at our marriage. In the Name of Jesus I pray.

Confession: I will work harder and stay committed to building a better home and marriage, not giving in to the devil who wants to destroy our marriage.

Day 10
The Power of Prayer

Confess your faults one to another, and pray one for another, that ye may be healed. The effectual fervent prayer of a righteous man availeth much (James 5:16).

There is nothing that can take the place of praying in faith on a daily basis for the person you are trying to win.

When a person prays, he gets God involved on the scene. Sometimes we don't pray for our marriage partners as much as we think we do. We pray many hours for everybody else, and everything else, forgetting to spend the needed time to pray for our own husband or wife, the one with whom we live the most intimately and upon whom we depend every day.

Prayer: Father, help me to spend time in prayer for my husband or wife. Help me to reach down in my heart and pray in faith for him or her. In the Name of Jesus I pray.

Confession: I receive help to pray for the one I love, and faith to stand with him or her.

Day 11
They Two Shall Be One

For this cause shall a man leave his father and mother, and shall be joined unto his wife, and they two shall be one flesh (Eph. 5:31).

Most people spend so much of their time earning a living that they forget to live.

Yes, we do need to work, but we also need to spend time with our families. This is vitally important to a healthy home and marriage. We need time together, to get to know the needs of each other. We need to fulfill that deep desire in the heart of our marriage partner that can only be filled by us alone.

There is a certain fellowship I can share with my wife that she cannot get from anyone else. This was ordained by God, as it was He who joined man and wife together.

Prayer: Father, help me to take time to love my wife or husband, and help me to take time to share with him or her. In the Name of Jesus I pray.

Confession: I confess that every day I desire my mate more and more, and I will take the time to share with him or her.

Day 12
First Things First

But seek ye first the kingdom of God, and his righteousness; and all these things shall be added unto you (Matt. 6:33)

"I don't have time." We hear that statement spoken nearly every day of our lives. Perhaps you have said it yourself thousands of times. "I don't have the time to spare for my family."

You will never have time, you will have to make the time. The devil knows that if he can get you to neglect your family long enough, it will fall apart. I learned a number of years ago that if a person doesn't take time for his family, it will never come.

If you will ask God, He will help you to find time. It will seem as if more hours have been added to the day, or your work will be done faster, or you will see that other things are just not that important.

Prayer: Father, help me with my time, so that I can be with my family, as I should.

Confession: I have time to be with my family, to set the example and show the love that I should.

Day 13
Say the Good Word

Heaviness in the heart of man maketh it stoop: but a good word maketh it glad (Prov. 12:25).

Whom do you remember and appreciate the most? Isn't it the person who tries to build you up and not tear you down?

We all need to be built up, not brought down. Everyone needs to be encouraged. We all need to be commended. This will go a long way toward building a great marriage. Most husbands and wives are too busy criticizing each other. Soon, so much criticism turns into hate and rebellion.

Your words of encouragement will create a closer unity in your marriage. It will take time, but if you will begin to speak words of encouragement and commendation, through patience you will begin to see the Holy Spirit at work in your marriage.

Prayer: Father, help me to build up my marriage, and not to tear it down by speaking words of discouragement. Give me words inspired by the Holy Spirit to speak to my mate. In the Name of Jesus I pray.

Confession: I will speak encouraging, inspiring words to build up my marriage.

Day 14
Patience

For ye have need of patience, that, after ye have done the will of God, ye might receive the promise (Heb. 10:36).

You may discover at this time there is still a lot of work to be done in your family, even in your own self.

This is nothing to get discouraged about, rather rejoice that you see the truth and are willing to change. Sometimes, if you will look closely, you will find that your patience with your family is shorter than with people outside of your home. This should not be. If there is anyone we should love, have patience with, be willing to teach and work with, it is our own family. If you can be kind to others, you can be kind to your own family members. Put Philippians 4:13 to work: *I can do all things through Christ which strengtheneth me.*

Prayer: Father, I repent of my lack of patience, of not trying as hard to work with my own family as I do with other people. In the Name of Jesus I pray.

Confession: I receive strength to be the person that I should be to my family. I can be kind and patient, because I receive strength to do it from Christ.

Day 15
Pray in the Spirit

But ye, beloved, building up yourselves on your most holy faith, praying in the Holy Ghost . . . (Jude 20).

The greatest thing you can do for your marriage and family is to pray for them in the Spirit. If you do not know how to do this, then you need to receive the Baptism in the Holy Ghost. Ask God to fill you with His Spirit with the evidence of speaking with other tongues.

Romans 8:26 states, *Likewise the Spirit also helpeth our infirmities: for we know not what we should pray for as we ought: but the Spirit itself maketh intercession for us with groanings which cannot be uttered.*

We do not know how to pray at times, so we should allow the Holy Spirit to pray through us. He knows how to pray and what to pray for to meet our need.

Prayer: Father, help me to pray in the Holy Spirit each day for my family. In the Name of Jesus I pray.

Confession: I will pray in the Holy Spirit, and let Him use me as He desires each day.

Day 16
Source of Love

And hope maketh not ashamed; because the love of God is shed abroad in our hearts by the Holy Ghost which is given unto us (Rom. 5:5).

You may say, "I find it hard to love my husband or wife." It is good that you admit to a wrong in our life, but through God that situation can be changed.

Love is in your heart. You may not feel it, but it is there nonetheless. It may be suppressed, but you can activate it by confessing that the Holy Spirit has put love in your heart.

Prayer: Father, help me to have a new love in my heart for my mate and family. In the Name of Jesus I pray.

Confession: I am receiving new love from God in my heart for my mate and family. I confess that it is beginning to flow all through our house.

Day 17
Get in Agreement

Can two walk together, except they be agreed? (Amos 3:3).

A lot of problems in marriage can be worked out if only the couple is willing to talk and then really listen to each other. A husband and wife should always be willing to talk things out. But it is not enough just to talk, they must be willing to listen to each other, keeping an open mind about what is said.

I have seen people whose minds were already closed before you talked to them. This can only block the working of God. Learn to listen, then be willing to pray and to follow the leadership of God's Holy Spirit in your marriage.

Prayer: Father, help me to be willing to talk and listen to my wife or husband, and then help me to seek Your face in prayer and to be willing to do whatever You show me to do. In the Name of Jesus I pray.

Confession: I receive wisdom to talk, to listen, and to pray that there may be a sweeter relationship in my marriage than ever before.

Day 18
Show Appreciation

The lips of the righteous know what is acceptable: but the mouth of the wicked speaketh frowardness (Prov. 10:32).

One thing that many married people fail to do is to look for new ways to improve themselves, their mate, and their marriage.

When a couple first meet, they go out of their way to be nice and polite to each other. But after they have been married for a while they begin dropping their guard. They start taking each other for granted. They forget to compliment each other.

A lot of hard work goes into making and keeping a home (caring for children, earning the living, washing dishes, mowing the grass, cleaning the house, keeping the cars clean and in good running order, doing the laundry, etc.) Learn to appreciate all the things your mate does for you and compliment him or her on it.

Prayer: Father, help me to appreciate my wife or husband for all the good things he or she does for me. In the Name of Jesus I pray.

Confession: I receive help from God to appreciate my mate more and to show my appreciation by complimenting him or her daily.

Day 19
Friendship in Marriage

Go home to thy friends . . . (Mark 5:19).

A person's best friends should be in his own home. Far too many married couples fail to learn how to be each other's best friend.

But friendship must be developed. Proverbs 18:24 says, *A man that hath friends is friendly.* Do you know how to win new friends? The Bible says you must show yourself friendly.

I have found that couples who not only love one another, but who also are each other's best friend, invariably have a marriage that is strong and enjoyable. They are able to confide in and have confidence in one another. They enjoy each other's company.

Prayer: Father, I ask You to help me not only to build love in our marriage, but also friendship. Help me to show myself friendly toward my companion, _____.

(call his/her name in prayer)

In the Name of Jesus I pray.

Confession: I will be friends with my partner, showing love and confidence in him or her.

Day 20
Making Decisions Together

If a house be divided against itself, that house cannot stand (Mark 3:25).

Married couples need to make decisions together as partners, understanding that major decisions will affect the whole family. Resentment, even hatred, will sometimes build up in one of the partners because he or she is left out of decision making. Some husbands and some wives, for example, will go out and buy things on credit, not consulting with their mate first, not thinking whether they can afford what is being charged or not, getting the family into debt. Such action can only lead to arguments and bitterness.

Too many couples will not spend the time needed together in prayer before a decision is made. If family decisions are based on the Word of God, they will be good for the entire family.

Prayer: Father, help me to take the time to involve my companion in my actions. Let us pray about the decisions we make. In the Name of Jesus I pray.

Confession: I confess that we pray and make decisions together, as we work together to build a better marriage.

Day 21
Jealousy

For jealousy is the rage of a man: therefore he will not spare in the day of vengeance (Prov. 6:34).

Jealousy is a rage. Husbands and wives need to beware of this dreadful enemy. Do not let it into your lives. Learn to trust each other, have faith in each other. This will build a stronger marriage.

I have seen men and women destroy beautiful marriages because of a jealous heart. Satan will talk to a person and put thoughts in his or her head that are not so. I have seen men get mad if they saw their wives talking to another man, even though the conversation was purely innocent.

My wife knows that as a minister I have to talk with other women all the time, but there is a trust there. As a minister's wife, she has to deal with all kinds of people, so we have both learned to trust each other, knowing that our work is for the glory of the Lord.

Prayer: Father, help me to rebuke the enemy of jealousy and to cast it out of my heart. In the Name of Jesus I pray.

Confession: I receive help to overcome jealousy and strength to place trust in my mate.

Day 22
Setting the Example

We then that are strong ought to bear the infirmities of the weak, and not to please ourselves (Rom. 15:1).

In a marriage, the stronger should set the example for the other to follow.

From my years of experience in counseling I have seen that many times in a marriage there is one partner who tries hard, while the other partner does not seem to really care. If this is your case, you must not give up. You must realize that you are fighting a spiritual warfare with the devil. God is on your side, you can win, but you must be willing to obey the instructions of God and pay the price for a better marriage. Part of that price is setting the example for your mate to follow.

Prayer: Father, help me to set an example for my marriage. Help me to pay the price to build a better marriage. In the Name of Jesus I pray.

Confession: I receive the grace and faith to follow the instructions of God, to set the example, and not to please myself.

Day 23
Casting Down Imaginations

Casting down imaginations, and every high thing that exalteth itself against the knowledge of God, and bringing into captivity every thought to the obedience of Christ (2 Cor. 10:5).

"The harder I try, it seems the worse our marriage becomes. Why try?"

If this expresses your feelings, you must cast such thoughts down. They are from Satan. The devil wants to build up in your mind the imagination that you cannot win, that there is no hope, no use in trying.

This is a direct attack upon the Word of God. God said, "Love never fails." If God has said something, you can count on it, it works. Keep on fighting the good fight of faith. You can take your marriage out of the hands of the devil. You can win because God is on your side.

Prayer: Father, help me to cast down imaginations, and to take on the mind of a winner. I can do all things through Christ who strengthens me. In the Name of Jesus I pray.

Confession: I confess that my marriage is free from the power of the devil. We are winners.

Day 24
Fight the Good Fight

But thanks be to God, which giveth us the victory through our Lord Jesus Christ (1 Cor. 15:57).

Anything worth having is worth fighting for, and every marriage is worth having. But wishing and doing and day dreaming will not get the job done. By using your faith, praying in the Spirit, and not giving up, you will see results.

If you think that the devil is going to sit still while you build a marriage that will glorify God, you are wrong. If my wife and I had not been willing to pay the price for success in the early years of our marriage, we would not have a marriage today. The devil threw everything he had at us, but praise God we were more than conquerors through Christ our Lord.

Prayer: Father, help me to use my faith; help me to take authority over the enemy who is trying to destroy our marriage.

Confession: I have power and authority over the enemy through our Lord Jesus Christ.

Day 25
Accentuate the Positive

Finally, brethren, whatsoever things are true, whatsoever things are honest, whatsoever things are just, whatsoever things are pure, whatsoever things are lovely, whatsoever things are of good report; if there be any virtue, and if there be any praise, think on these things (Phil. 4:8).

Find the good things in your marriage and mate, look for the best and not for the worst. You may say, "But there is nothing good in the person that I have married." Sometimes through a period of time, a person begins to see only the negative side and not the positive. You will usually find what you are looking for, if you look long and hard enough. If you look for faults, you will find them, because no person and no marriage is perfect.

Begin to look for the good things in your marriage and mate. The more you look, the more you will find.

Prayer: Father, help me to look and think on the good things in our marriage. In the Name of Jesus I pray.

Confession: I can, through Christ, overcome a negative life and look at my mate and marriage through the eyes of love.

Day 26
The God-Kind of Love

There is a friend that sticketh closer than a brother (Prov. 18:24).

God sees deep down on the inside of us. He sees all of our mistakes, all of our faults. But He still loves us and wants our fellowship.

This is one of the greatest revelations I have ever received. God knows all about me, but He still loves me and wants to fellowship with me. It goes even deeper than that. Romans 5:8 says, *While we were yet sinners, Christ died for us.* If Almighty God, a perfect and upright God, so loved us, knowing all about our sins and faults, how much more should we be willing to love and forgive one another?

Husbands and wives need this God-kind of love in their homes.

Prayer: Father, help us to have Your kind of love for each other. Help us to have the God-kind of love. In the Name of Jesus I pray.

Confession: I confess that God is filling our hearts with His God-kind of love for each other.

Day 27
The Undefiled Bed

Marriage is honourable in all, and the bed undefiled: but whoremongers and adulterers God will judge (Heb. 13:4).

The marriage bed has been ordained by God to enrich the love and fellowship of each marriage. But many marriages are destroyed or never have the rich enjoyment that God has intended, because people sometimes think sex is something dirty. Yet it was God who created and ordained sex. But He reserved it exclusively for man and his wife.

A husband and wife can never be at perfect peace unless there is a good sex life between them. There is a hunger in each heart that can only be filled by this part of marriage.

Prayer: Father, help me to yield my life to this part of Your plan for a man and wife; help me to fulfill the need in my husband or wife's life. Help us to close the door to the devil so that he cannot take advantage of a weak link in our relationship.

Confession: I enjoy the sexual relationship that God has ordained between me and my companion, and a deeper desire grows daily between us.

Day 28
Ravished With Love

Let her be as the loving hind and pleasant roe; let her breasts satisfy thee at all times; and be thou ravished always with her love (Prov. 5:19).

Here are instructions from God concerning the sexual relationship in a marriage. Notice these words: loving, pleasant, satisfy, ravished. Obviously sex plays a great part in a marriage, whether a person wants to admit it or not.

Learn to be concerned about your mate's sexual need. It is your responsibility to fulfill that need always and at all times. You may say, "But he (or she) will take advantage of me." No, your submission will cause your love for each other to grow; and where love grows, fellowship and consideration will also grow.

A husband and wife must learn to satisfy each other by their love for one another, and sex is one way in which that love is nurtured and increased.

Prayer: Father, help me not to have the wrong attitude about our sex life, but let this be a pleasant time of fellowship together. In the Name of Jesus I pray.

Confession: We receive help from God to build a better sex life in our marriage.

Day 29
Defraud Not the Other

The wife hath not power of her own body, but the husband: and likewise also the husband hath not power of his own body, but the wife. Defraud ye not one the other, except it be with consent for a time, that ye may give yourselves to fasting and prayer; and come together again, that Satan tempt you not for your incontinency (1 Cor. 7:4-5).

It is unscriptural for a husband and wife to withhold sex from each other. The Word of God says that they should refrain only with consent, and then only for a time of fasting and prayer. Afterwards they should come together again so that Satan will not tempt them.

I have counseled with couples who were using sex as a weapon against each other to get even about something. Such people always end up in arguments and with heartaches. Look at sex in the marriage as pure and undefiled. Work together to build a healthy sex life.

Prayer: Help us to love each other, to fulfill each other's needs as You have commanded. Help us to build a better marriage. In the Name of Jesus I pray.

Confession: I confess that God is involved in our marriage, working out His glory in us through Christ Jesus our Lord and Savior.

Day 30
Wisdom:
Foundation of Marriage

If any of you lack wisdom, let him ask of God, that giveth to all men liberally, and upbraideth not; and it shall be given him (James 1:5).

We must understand that marriage must be founded upon the Word of God. It must be built upon a proper relationship between the marriage partners and with God.

Don't give up on your marriage. Get God involved in your problems. He has the wisdom you need, and will give it to you. He will not hold back anything from you.

You must remember that God wants to help you and your marriage to be a total success. To pull your marriage out of difficulty will take time. You must be patient and let God help you each day.

Prayer: Father, I ask You to give me wisdom and insight about how to build a better marriage each day. In the Name of Jesus I pray.

Confession: I receive wisdom from God each day of my life to help me build a better marriage.

PRAYER OF SALVATION

God loves you—no matter who you are, no matter what your past. God loves you so much that He gave His one and only begotten Son for you. The Bible tells us that "...whoever believes in him shall not perish but have eternal life" (John 3:16 NIV). Jesus laid down His life and rose again so that we could spend eternity with Him in heaven and experience His absolute best on earth. If you would like to receive Jesus into your life, say the following prayer out loud and mean it from your heart.

Heavenly Father, I come to You admitting that I am a sinner. Right now, I choose to turn away from sin, and I ask You to cleanse me of all unrighteousness. I believe that Your Son, Jesus, died on the cross to take away my sins. I also believe that He rose again from the dead so that I might be forgiven of my sins and made righteous through faith in Him. I call upon the name of Jesus Christ to be the Savior and Lord of my life. Jesus, I choose to follow You and ask that You fill me with the power of the Holy Spirit. I declare that right now I am a child of God. I am free from sin and full of the righteousness of God. I am saved in Jesus' name. Amen

If you prayed this prayer to receive Jesus Christ as your Savior for the first time, please contact us on the web at www.harrisonhouse.com to receive a free book.

Or you may write to us at
Harrison House Publishers
P.O. Box 35035
Tulsa, Oklahoma 74153

ABOUT THE AUTHOR

After accepting Christ in 1969, Donald Moore filled many roles in the ministry of helps. In 1973 he attended the Baptist Bible College in Springfield, Missouri. Shortly afterwards, he established a church in his home state of North Carolina.

While pastoring his first church, Donald became hungry for an even deeper relationship with God. He then received the Baptism of the Holy Spirit. Donald has since pastored three more full-gospel churches and is now an evangelist with the Assemblies of God. His home is in Charlotte, North Carolina.

For ministry inquiries or personal counseling needs write to:

Donald E. Moore
STEPS TO VICTORY MINISTRIES, INC.
P.O. Box 221316
Charlotte, NC 28222-1316

Additional copies of this book are
available from your local bookstore

HARRISON HOUSE
Tulsa, Oklahoma 74153

If this book has been a blessing to you
or if you would like to see more of the
Harrison House product line,
please visit us on our website at
www.harrisonhouse.com

The Harrison House Vision

Proclaiming the truth and the power
Of the Gospel of Jesus Christ
With excellence;

Challenging Christians to
Live victoriously,
Grow spiritually,
Know God intimately.